LIBRARIANS

HELP US FIND INFORMATION

Grateful acknowledgment is made to
Cornelius O'Shea
Assistant Regional Director
The Chicago Public Library
Sulzer Regional Library
and Marci A. LaZar
Irving Park Middle School

Photo Credits:
All photos © Phil Martin

Library of Congress Cataloging-in-Publication Data

Greene, Carol.

Librarians help us find information/by Carol Greene.
    p.   cm.
Includes index.
Summary: Simple text and photographs describe what librarians do.
Concludes with a question and answer section.
ISBN 1-56766-558-6 (lib. bdg. : alk. paper)
1. Library science—United States—Juvenile literature. 2. Public
libraries—United States—Juvenile literature. [1. LIbrarians.
2. Libraries. 3. Occupations.] I. Title.

Z665.5.G77   1998   98-20331
027—dc21   CIP
    AC

LIBRARIANS
HELP US FIND INFORMATION

By Carol Greene

The Child's World®, Inc.

SHHH!

It's morning in the **library**.
People come here to read books
and learn about things.

CLICK! CLICK!

Librarians turn on the lights and
computers. They unlock the
doors, too. Soon the library will
be open.

CLUMP! CLUMP!

Mr. Jones is always first. He likes
to read magazines at the library.
He also likes to read newspapers.

The children's librarian puts new books on the shelf.

THUMP! THUMP!

A class is coming to visit. How can they find the books they want? The children's librarian will show them. Then she will read them a story.

This is the head librarian. He uses his computer to order new books.

TAP! TAP! TAP!

He orders tapes and CDs, too. Many people borrow music from the library.

"Do you have a map of Africa?"
asks a woman.

"Oh yes," says the librarian.
"Let me get it for you."
Librarians must know where
everything is in the library.

BRRRING!

A boy calls on the telephone. He has a question about baseball.

"Who won the World Series in 1942?" he asks.

The librarian looks up the answer in a book. Librarians must know where to find **information**.

"I need a book about raising chickens," says a man. "But I don't know how to work the computer. Can you help me?"

The librarian helps the man.

TAP! TAP!

Many libraries list their books on a computer.

"This library doesn't have any books about raising chickens," says the librarian. "Let me check another library."

The other library has just the right book. They will send it over.

Sometimes people cannot come to the library. The librarians try to bring them some books instead.

Every week, this librarian takes books to a **nursing home**. She gives them to the people who live there. When they are finished reading them, she takes them back to the library.

TOOT! TOOT!

A delivery man brings some new children's books. They are packed in big brown boxes.

THUMP!

He gives the books to a librarian.

The librarian looks at the books. She puts information about each book into the computer. Then she puts a special sticker on each book. Each book has a number or letter code.

Then she puts each book on the shelf. Each kind of book has its own special place in the library.

"Do you have a book about pilots?" asks a boy.

"Yes! I'll show you where to find it," says the librarian. "Here it is."

These librarians look through a stack of books. Some have torn and dirty covers. They will be mended and put back on the shelves. The librarians take good care of the books. They take care of the videos, magazines, and CDs, too.

The daytime librarian is going home now.
Now it is the evening librarian's turn. She will
help people find the information they need.

QUESTIONS AND ANSWERS

What do librarians do?

Librarians work with books and other materials. They help people find information. Some work in public libraries or school libraries. Others work for businesses, hospitals, or universities. Some drive library vans called "bookmobiles."

How do people learn to be librarians?

Most librarians go to college for four years. They study many different subjects. Then they go to graduate school for at least another year. There they study library science. Library technical assistants (LTAs) go to college for a year or two.

What kind of people are librarians?

Librarians must be smart and organized. They must like books and information. Most of all, they must like people. Helping people is their main job.

How much money do librarians make?

Librarians who work for the federal government make about $41,200 a year. Librarians working in small libraries make about $24,000 a year. Bigger library systems can pay their librarians more than small library systems.

GLOSSARY

computer (kom–PYOO–ter)
A computer is a special machine that holds information. It also gives answers quickly.

information (in–for–MAY–shun)
Information is facts about something. Librarians can help you find all kinds of information.

library (LIE–brer–ee)
A library is a building that holds books, magazines, and newspapers for people to use.

nursing home (NUR–sing HOME)
A nursing home is a place where people can live if they need help doing things. Many older people live in nursing homes.

INDEX

CDs, II, 29

children's librarian, 9

computer, II, I7

computers, 5

delivery man, 23

head librarian, II

helping, I3, I5, I7, I9, 2I, 27

library, 5

magazines, 7

mending, 29

newspapers, 7

nursing home, 2I

questions and answers, 3I

tapes, II

CAROL GREENE has published over 200 books for children. She also likes to read books, make teddy bears, work in her garden, and sing. Ms. Greene lives in Webster Groves, Missouri.